Newcastle Elementary School
8400 136th Ave. SE
Newcastle, WA 98059
425-837-5825

How Does Your Heart Work?

By Don L. Curry

Consultants
Jayne Waddell, MA, RN, LPC
School Nurse, Health Educator, Counselor

Jeanne Clidas, Ph.D.
National Reading Consultant and Professor of Reading
SUNY Brockport

Children's Press®
A Division of Scholastic Inc.
New York   Toronto   London   Auckland   Sydney
Mexico City   New Delhi   Hong Kong
Danbury, Connecticut

Designer: Herman Adler Design
Photo Researcher: Caroline Anderson
The photo on the cover shows a simple view of the circulatory system.

Library of Congress Cataloging-in-Publication Data

Curry, Don L.
  How does you heart work? / Don L. Curry.– 1st American ed.
    p. cm. – (Rookie read-about health)
  Includes index.
  Summary: Provides a simple introduction to how the heart and circulatory
system work.
    ISBN 0-516-25861-3 (lib. bdg.)   0-516-27855-X (pbk.)
  1. Heart–Juvenile literature. 1. Heart. 2. Circulatory system.]
  I. Title. II. Series.
  QP111.6.C87 2004
  612.1'7–dc21
                                          2003003916

CHILDREN'S PRESS, and ROOKIE READ-ABOUT®,
and associated logos are trademarks and or registered trademarks
of Scholastic Library Publishing. SCHOLASTIC and associated logos
are trademarks and or registered trademarks of Scholastic Inc.

1 2 3 4 5 6 7 8 9 10 R 12 11 10 09 08 07 06 05 04 03

Have you ever given
someone a heart?

Your heart does not really look the way we see it in cards or pictures. It looks more like this:

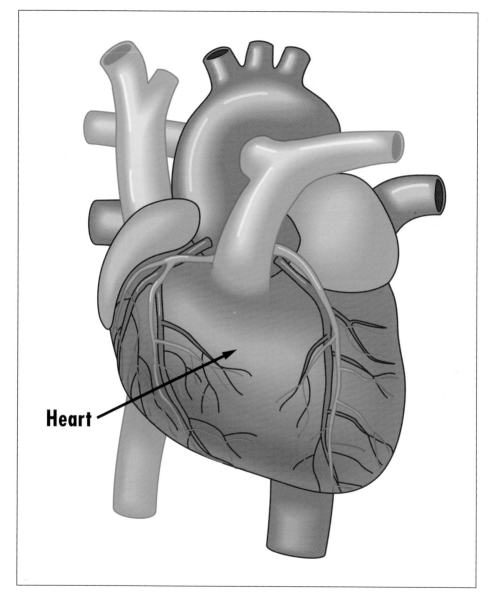

Heart

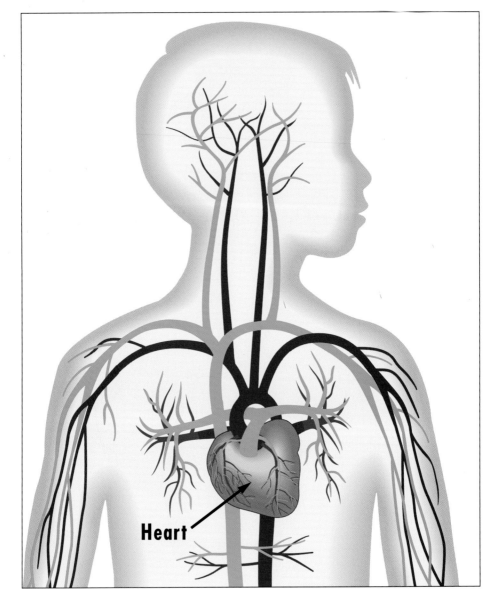

Heart

Your heart is inside your chest. Your heart keeps blood moving inside your body.

Your heart is about
the size of your fist.
As you grow bigger,
so will your heart.

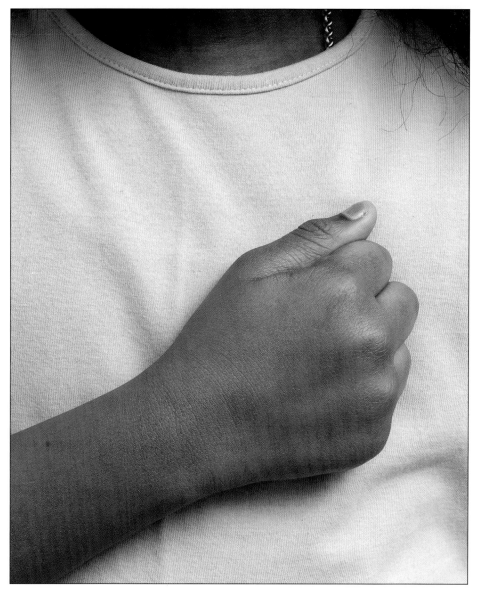

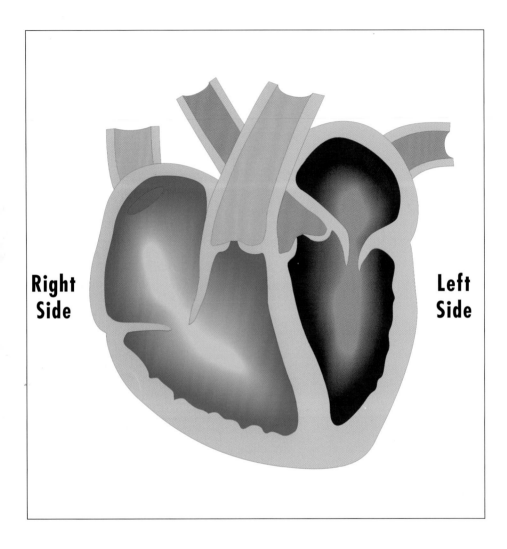

**Right
Side**

**Left
Side**

Your heart is made up of two pumps sitting side by side. The pumps are made of muscle.

Inside your heart there are four small rooms called chambers (CHAME-burs).

There are two chambers on each side of your heart.

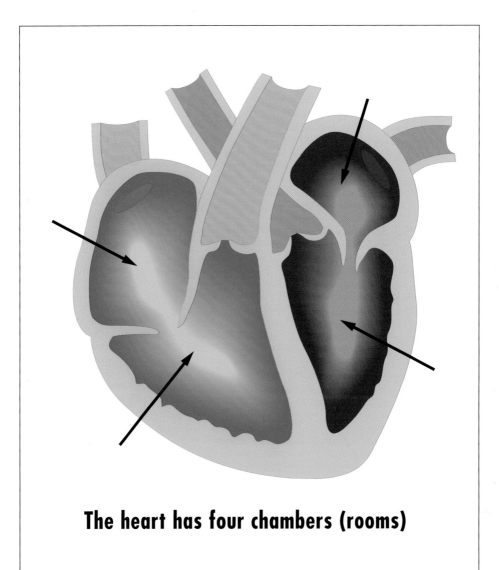

The heart has four chambers (rooms)

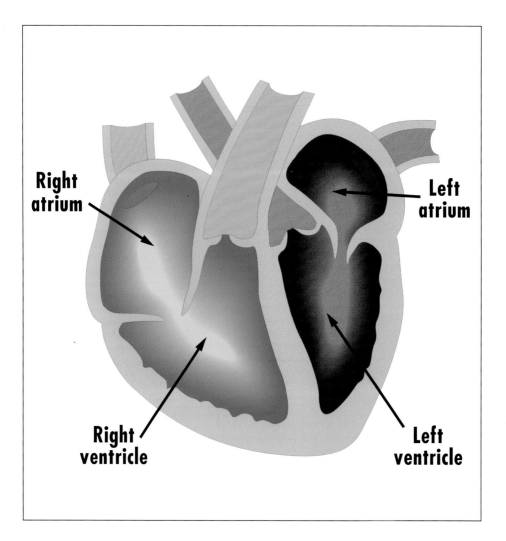

Right
atrium

Left
atrium

Right
ventricle

Left
ventricle

14

The chambers at the top of your heart are called the right atrium (AY-tree-uhm) and the left atrium.

The chambers at the bottom of you heart are called the right ventricle (VEN-truh-kuhl) and the left ventricle.

The chambers on the right
side of your heart take
in blood that has already
moved through your body.

The blood coming back
to the heart from your body
is blue because it has no
oxygen (OK-suh-juhn).

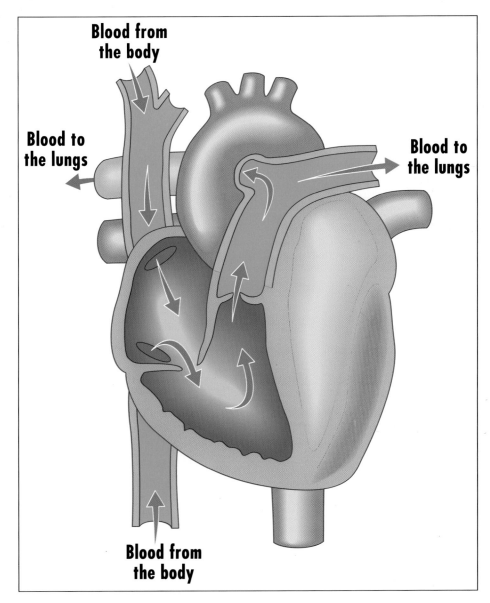

Blood from the body

Blood to the lungs

Blood to the lungs

Blood from the body

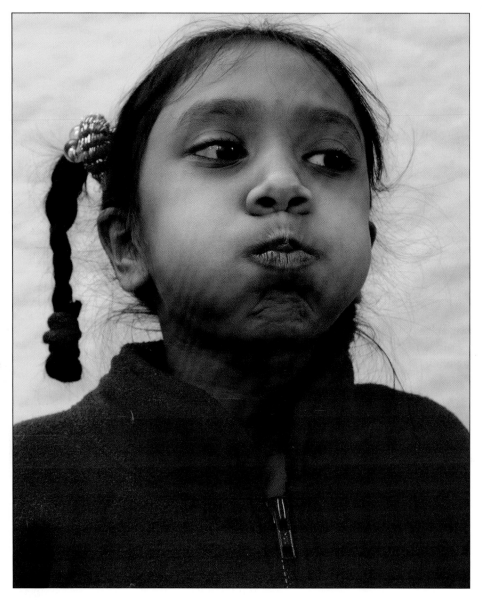

18

Each time you breathe,
your lungs fill with oxygen.

The heart pumps the
blue blood to your lungs
to take in oxygen.

When it gets oxygen,
the blood turns red.

The red blood is pumped into the chambers on the left side of your heart.

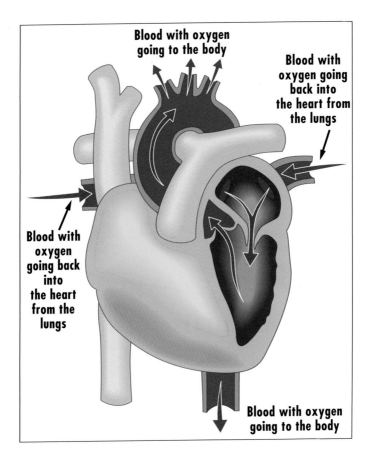

Blood with oxygen going to the body

Blood with oxygen going back into the heart from the lungs

Blood with oxygen going back into the heart from the lungs

Blood with oxygen going to the body

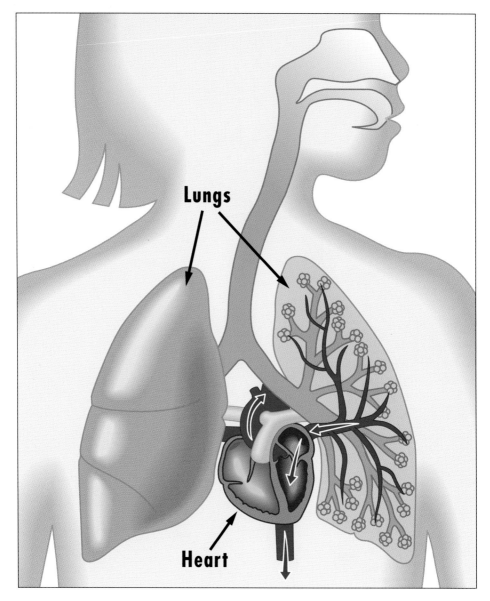

Lungs

Heart

21

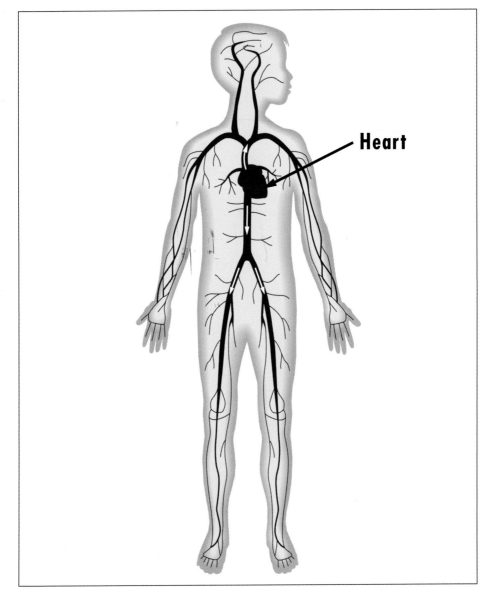

Heart

Your heart then pumps the blood with oxygen out to the rest of your body.

Your blood also carries nutrients (NOO-tree-uhnts) to give you energy. Your body would stop working if it didn't have oxygen or nutrients.

The blood flows through rubbery tubes called blood vessels.

If you see dark lines that look like spider webs under your skin, those are your blood vessels.

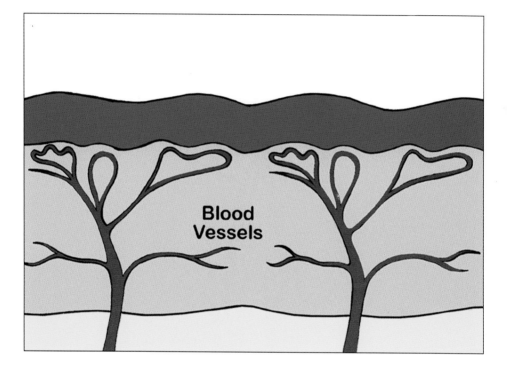

Blood
Vessels

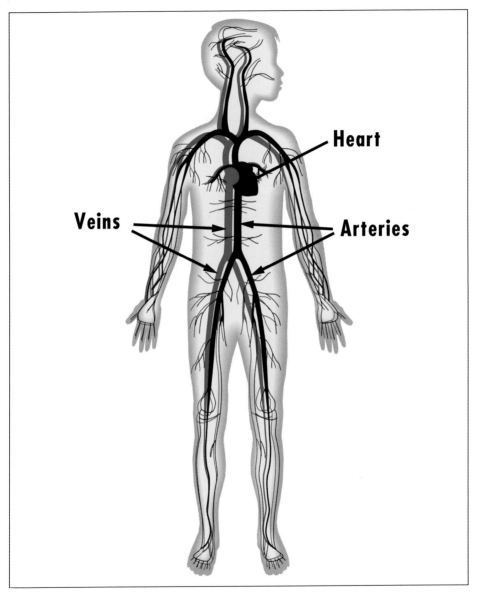

Heart

Veins

Arteries

The blood vessels that carry blood away from your heart are called arteries.

The blood vessels that carry blood from your body into your heart are called veins.

It is important to have
a healthy heart.

Exercising, eating healthy
foods, and resting will
keep your heart healthy.

Words You Know

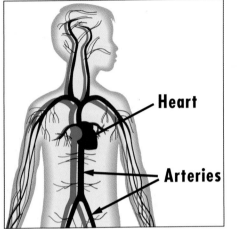

arteries

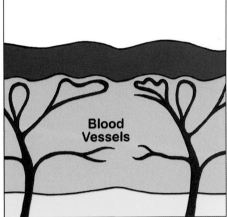
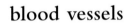

blood vessels

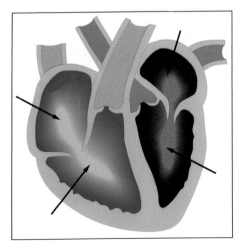

heart chambers

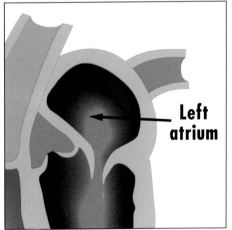

left atrium

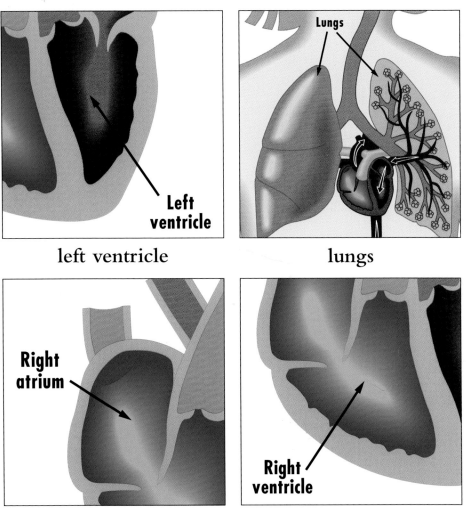

left ventricle

lungs

right atrium

right ventricle

Index

About the Author

Don L. Curry is a writer, editor, and educational consultant who lives and works in New York City. When he is not writing, Don can generally be found in the park reading, or riding his bike exploring the streets of "the greatest city on earth."

Photo Credits

Photographs © 2003: Custom Medical Stock Photo: 25 (Educational Images); Ellen B. Senisi: 9, 18 Photo Researchers, NY: 29 (PH Royer); PhotoEdit: 3 (Richard Hutchings).

Illustrations by Bob Italiano